The Lord's Instructions

FOR NEW MEMBERS OF
THE CHURCH OF JESUS CHRIST
OF LATTER-DAY SAINTS

Other Books by Thomas E. Johnson:

Life's Three Greatest Questions

The Lord's Instructions

for New Members of The Church of Jesus Christ of Latter-day Saints

By
Thomas E. Johnson

CFI

Springville, Utah

ISBN: 1-55517-773-5
e. 1

Published by Cedar Fort Inc.
www.cedarfort.com

Distributed by:

Cover design by Nicole Shaffer
Cover design © 2004 by Lyle Mortimer

Printed in the United States of America
10 9 8 7 6 5 4 3 2 1
Printed on acid-free paper

Library of Congress Control Number: 2004110392

INTRODUCTION

You are a new member of The Church of Jesus Christ of Latter-day Saints! You should be excited about this new step you have taken in your life—a giant step in spiritual progress. Perhaps you were introduced to the Church by family members or by neighbors. Or maybe you were one of those special people who answered the knock at the door and permitted the missionaries to come into your home to teach you the gospel of Jesus Christ as restored through the prophet Joseph Smith.

Through the missionary discussions you learned the basic doctrines of the Church. In addition, at Church meetings you observed the members and the practices of the Church. You read the scriptures and learned the importance of believing in the Lord Jesus Christ, conforming your lifestyle to His teachings (which we call repentance), receiving baptism for the remission of your past sins, and receiving the Holy Ghost to guide you in your life.

You learned to pray to your Father in Heaven and began to experience inspiration through the Holy Ghost. Through all this you probably had repeated meetings with the missionaries. There may have been others who took an interest in your progress as you studied about the Church. Hopefully, you have met the bishop of your ward, the Elders Quorum President, the Relief Society President, and other ward leaders and members whom you will come to know and love.

As a new member of the Church, you should receive the "New Member Discussions" from the missionaries or the members. These, like the missionary discussions you heard before joining the Church, are designed to broaden and deepen your knowledge of the gospel and Church doctrines. Sometimes it may seem like there is a lot to learn and the task can be daunting, even overwhelming. Fortunately, the Lord has said that it is not necessary for you to run faster than you have strength,[1] but He has commanded you to be diligent and to

---

1. Mosiah 4:27, The Book of Mormon; Doctrine & Covenants 10:4.

continue to learn "line upon line, precept upon precept, here a little and there a little."[2] As you continue to study and learn, you will come to know all that is important to bless your life here and to prepare you for immortality and eternal life.

As a new member of the Church you may receive advice from many people. The missionaries who taught you probably added some of their own personal advice beyond the specific information they were asked to teach you. At your baptism, those who spoke probably offered their advice on how to progress in the Church. As a new member of the Church you should have home teachers and visiting teachers to visit and befriend you, answer your questions, and encourage you in your new faith.

All of this advice is good. Each person who offers you advice is well-meaning and has had experiences from which he or she has gained his or her perspective. Probably all members of the Church emphasize certain doctrines or

2. Isaiah 28:10, 2 Nephi 28:30, The Book of Mormon, Doctrine & Covenants 98:12, 128:21.

practices which have been influential in their faith and testimony. You will also develop special feelings toward certain doctrines or practices that are especially meaningful to you in the same way.

However, in addition to the advice that is given to you by many different people, you should consider a very special revelation given by the Lord through the Prophet Joseph Smith to Sidney Gilbert, a new member of the Church. In this revelation, the Lord told Brother Gilbert the things he should do to gain his exaltation and eternal life. We will review that revelation, verse by verse, to seek to understand the instruction the Lord gave to him.

Sidney Gilbert—The Lord's Pattern for New Members of the Church

God the Father and His Son Jesus Christ appeared to Joseph Smith in 1820 when Joseph was only 14 years old. At that time, Jesus Christ told Joseph that he needed to receive further instruction before he would be ready to restore and lead the true Church of Jesus Christ. Three years later, when Joseph was 17, his first instruction began under the tutelage of Moroni, the resurrected ancient prophet who had compiled and buried the writings which would comprise the Book of Mormon. This instruction continued annually for the next four years. Joseph then translated and published the Book of Mormon. Other heavenly messengers, including John the Baptist and the ancient Apostles—Peter, James, and John—restored the Aaronic and Melchizedek Priesthood authority to Joseph

Smith and Oliver Cowdery. With that priesthood they organized The Church of Jesus Christ of Latter-day Saints on April 6, 1830, in upstate New York.

Missionaries worked to spread the news of the restoration of the gospel of Jesus Christ. One of the people who heard the gospel message was Algernon Sidney Gilbert.[3] Sidney was born in 1789 in New Haven, Connecticut. By 1817 he was living in Ohio and was engaged in operating a small store. When the missionaries passed through that area in November of 1830, he heard and accepted the gospel. As a new member of the Church, Sidney wondered what the Lord would have him do. Not long afterward, Joseph Smith, the young prophet of the Church—only 25 at that time—relocated from New York to Ohio with the other Church leaders. Sidney then

3. The biographical information on Brother Gilbert's life comes from *History of the Church of Jesus Christ of Latter-day Saints*, Vol. 1, pp. 145 (footnote), 179, 188, 391, 394, 432, Vol. 2, pp. 112, 113, 118-19 (footnote), Doctrine & Covenants 57:8-10, 61:7-12, 64:8, 82:11-12, 90:35, 101:96, and *Who's Who in the Doctrine & Covenants*. Bookcraft: Salt Lake City Utah, 1997. pp. 102-04.

had the opportunity to ask the Prophet this question directly.

In a remarkable revelation, now recorded as Section 53 in The Doctrine and Covenants, the Lord Jesus Christ answered Sidney's question. However, this revelation was more than an answer for Sidney alone. In just seven short verses it contained a blueprint for every new member of the Church. There is no doubt that the Lord intended that this revelation be studied by all new members of the Church. The Prophet Nephi in the Book of Mormon said, "I did liken all scripture unto us that it might be for our profit and learning."[4] This is certainly applicable to the revelation given to Sidney Gilbert. Every new member of the Church can attain exaltation and eternal life by accepting the Lord's instruction in this brief revelation.

_____

4. 1 Nephi 19:23.

1

I Have Heard Your Prayers
D&C 53:1

1. Behold, I say unto you, my servant Sidney Gilbert, that I have heard your prayers; and you have called upon me that it should be made known unto you, of the Lord your God, concerning your calling and election in the church, which I, the Lord, have raised up in these last days.

In the first verse of the Lord's revelation to Brother Gilbert we learn many things. The Lord calls Brother Gilbert by name, showing that He knows him personally. He also called him His "servant" because of his obedience in being baptized a member of the Church. He testified that the Church, which Brother Gilbert had joined, had been raised up by the Lord himself, through the instrumentality of the Prophet Joseph Smith and other leaders called by the Lord. But most importantly, the Lord confirmed that He had heard the prayers of Brother Gilbert asking about his calling and election in the Church. This reassurance from the Lord became a source of comfort and confidence for Brother Gilbert and for all members of the Church.

This verse of the revelation reminds you that as a new member of the Church you need to continue to seek the Lord's guidance through prayer. Jesus Christ taught, "Seek and ye shall find; knock and it shall be opened unto you."[5] Just as you did to find out if this Church is the true Church of God on the earth, you must continue to ask God for guidance in the other decisions you make in your life.

Sometimes, new members of the Church may question the power or ability of the Lord to hear everyone's prayers, or they may feel that their concerns are not important enough to be heard by the Lord. Sometimes, they think that only the Prophet or the Apostles of the Church can communicate with the Lord effectively. Other new members may expect a personal visitation from the Father and the

5. Luke 11:9.

Son, as Joseph Smith had, to answer questions or give them guidance in their lives. This revelation confirmed to Brother Gilbert that the Lord did hear his prayers, and you can take comfort and have confidence that the Lord hears your prayers.

One of the most instructive examples in the scriptures of the Lord's power is when He shared some of His power with the Prophet Moses. In the Pearl of Great Price we read:

. . . Blessed art thou, Moses, for I, the Almighty, have chosen thee, and thou shalt be made stronger than many waters; For they shall obey thy command as if thou wert God.

And lo, I am with thee, even unto the end of thy days; for thou shalt deliver my people from bondage, even Israel my chosen.

And it came to pass, as the voice was still speaking, Moses cast his eyes and beheld the earth, yea, even all of it; and there was not a particle of it which he did not behold, discerning it by the Spirit of God.

And he beheld also the inhabitants thereof,

and there was not a soul which he beheld not; and he discerned them by the Spirit of God; and their numbers were great, even number- less as the sand upon the sea shore.

And he beheld many lands; and each land was called earth, and there were inhabitants on the face thereof.[6]

From this we learn that Moses, as a prophet called by God, was given power to see every person on the earth at the same time, even though they were as numerous as the "sand upon the sea shore." The fact that Moses could enjoy such power for even a brief time can give us confidence that God, our Heavenly Father, can be aware of each of His children at all times. He can hear our prayers and know the thoughts and intents of our hearts, as well as our actions, and, when appropriate, can respond to our needs.

When Oliver Cowdery was trying to deter- mine whether Joseph Smith was indeed a prophet and whether he should act as a scribe

---

6. Moses 1: 25-29, The Pearl of Great Price, p. 3. See also Moses 1:8.

to assist Joseph in translating the Book of Mormon, he sought God in prayer. In a revelation that Jesus Christ then gave to Joseph Smith, He revealed to Joseph things that were only known by God and Oliver Cowdery. Jesus Christ told Oliver that the revelation to Joseph Smith should be accepted by Oliver as a demonstration that Joseph was God's appointed prophet.7

At another time, a man named Robert Smith recorded the following incident relating to Heber C. Kimball, one of the early Apostles of the Church:

> In 1857, I was working for Brother Heber and asked him for some goods, which he refused to let me have. Feeling bad over it, I went home and laid the matter before the Lord [in prayer]. The next morning when I came to work, Brother Heber called me into his room and said, 'Robert, what have you been complaining to the Lord for, about his servant Heber? Here

7. Doctrine & Covenants 6:15-24.

are the things you asked me for, and after this don't go to the Lord about every little thing that happens.'[8]

From these examples we can gain greater confidence that the Lord does hear us and, even though He may not always immediately answer our prayers, or give us the things we seek, it is of great benefit to know He listens. If He does not answer immediately or dramatically, it may be that there is more study and investigation needed on our part before the Lord will give us an answer or confirm to us that the decision we have made is in accordance with His will.[9] This is the Lord's way of developing our capabilities and giving us greater confidence to make decisions. He has told us that we should not have to be commanded in all things; that we should do many things of our own free will and bring to pass righteousness because the power is in us.[10] Sometimes the Lord's answer is "no." We need

8. Orson F. Whitney, Life of Heber C. Kimball (Bookcraft: Salt Lake City 1945)
9. Doctrine & Covenants 9:8.
10. Doctrine & Covenants 58:26-28

to accept that it is sometimes better for us if the thing we are seeking does not come to pass, for reasons only He knows.

Sometimes we have disobeyed the Lord and offended Him. He tells us that sometimes He withdraws Himself from us and through this we can understand that we need to repent in order to regain that personal relationship.[11] By continuing to pray, we may learn what we have done to offend Him and what we need to do to repent.

Sometimes we may not feel like praying. The Lord has commanded us that we should "pray always."[12] He has commanded us to pray vocally, for example, when asked to do so at our Church meetings,[13] and "in secret," for example, in our homes.[14] Brigham Young, the second President of the Church, taught that if we don't feel like praying, we should pray until we do feel like praying.[15] He also taught that if we don't receive a clear answer to our prayer,

---

11. Doctrine & Covenants 101:7-8.
12. Luke 18:1, Doctrine & Covenants 88:126, 101:81.
13. Doctrine & Covenants 19:28, 23:6.
14. Mathew 6:6.
15. Discourses of Brigham Young (John A. Widtsoe)(Deseret Book Company 1976), p. 44.

we should go forward using our best judgment, relying on the Lord to let us know if we are choosing correctly.[16] We also need to realize that some decisions do not affect our eternal salvation and the Lord can bless us whichever course we choose.[17]

In summary, we should always remember that our spiritual progress throughout our lives depends on seeking prayerful guidance from our Father in Heaven in the name of his son Jesus Christ.

---

16. Id. p. 43.
17. Doctrine & Covenants 58:26-28, 60:5, 61:22, 62:5, 63:40, 80:3.

2 Forsake the World
D&C 53:2

2.Behold, I, the Lord, who was crucified for the sins of the world, give unto you a commandment that you shall forsake the world.

The Lord Jesus Christ reminds Brother Gilbert that He was crucified for the sins of the world. The salvation of all depends upon this great event, known as the Atonement of Jesus Christ. The sins we committed were forgiven on the day of our baptism, but we can still sin by disregarding our weaknesses and succumbing to temptation, allowing ourselves to be tempted. Because of sin, we become impure, unworthy, and unable to return to the presence of God. Because Jesus Christ was the only sinless man that ever lived on the earth, God the Father agreed to accept Jesus' suffering and atonement in satisfaction for the personal suffering we each would have had to endure, provided we accept Jesus Christ and keep His commandments.[18]

Because we are all dependent upon the Atonement to achieve salvation and return to the presence of God the Father, Jesus has the right and authority to command us to do certain things to qualify for that blessing. In this revelation He commands Brother Gilbert and all of the members of the Church to "forsake the world."

What did He mean? One thing we know is that He was not telling Brother Gilbert to join a monastery or become a hermit. The Lord wants us to be a good influence in the world—a light unto the world,[19] the salt of the earth,[20] and the leaven of the loaf.[21] Additionally, each Sunday the Lord wants us to physically withdraw from the world to assemble for worship. But, from other scriptures it becomes clear the Lord is speaking of spiritually withdrawing from the world by forsaking the evil of the

---

18. Doctrine & Covenants 19:15-19.
19. Matthew 5:14-16.
20. Matthew 5:13.
21. Matthew 13:33.

world. In a very important section of scripture, the parable of the sower,[22] the Lord instructed the Apostles in the different ways that people fail to achieve salvation. In one example, He tells of those who accept the gospel (are baptized), but their growth is choked out by the cares of the world.[23] In another example, the Prophet Lehi was taught of the exquisite taste of the fruit of the Tree of Life, but he was shown that there were many who would not go forth and partake of it because they could not withstand the ridicule and scorn of the worldly.[24]

In reality, among those that join the Church, many fall away. Although the Lord told us this would happen, it is always a great sorrow to see it occur. One of the greatest causes for such falling away is the unwillingness of new members to completely and fully embrace the Church and the gospel. For many, to embrace the Church and the gospel means finding new friends who are members of the Church and who share the same faith in God and the goal of

22. Matthew 13.
23. Matthew 13:23.
24. 1 Nephi 8:26-28, The Book of Mormon.

obedience to His commandments. It means breaking old habits and replacing them with better habits. It means no longer seeking the praise of the world or worldly honors in preference to the honors and blessings that God desires to bestow upon us. For some this is too great a sacrifice. They wish to have some of the blessings of the gospel but keep parts of their old lifestyle. The Lord commands—not just suggests or recommends—that Brother Gilbert forsake the world, or "Babylon," as it is sometimes known in the scriptures, so he can pursue the Kingdom of Heaven. The Lord commands this because He knows that a "double-minded man is unstable in all his ways"[25] and that "no man can serve two masters."[26] He is telling Brother Gilbert to put his hand to the plow and not look back.[27] If he seeks to please men rather than God, he will fail in his pursuit of salvation. We must seek to please God. Our Church leaders have told us we must be "*in* the world, but not *of* the world."

25. James 1:8.
26. Mathew 6:24.
27. Luke 9:62.

3

Receive the Melchizedek Priesthood and Be a Missionary
D&C 53:3

3. Take upon you mine ordination, even that of an elder, to preach faith and repentance and remission of sins, according to my word, and the reception of the Holy Spirit by the laying on of hands.

To further progress, the Lord commands Brother Gilbert to prepare for and receive the ordination of Elder in the Melchizedek Priesthood. When a man or young man is baptized in the Church, he should first accept the preparatory or Aaronic Priesthood. As you learned when you studied to join the Church, the priesthood is the authority of God, including the authority of men on the earth to perform ordinances (religious cere-monies) that are accepted by God. One of the most important of those ordinances is baptism. It is extremely important that baptism be performed by proper priesthood authority; otherwise, the expected blessing of remission (forgiveness) of sins will not occur.

The priesthood is also the foundation of the government of the Church and the family. As a new member, accepting the priesthood is an expression of your desire to continue to learn and understand the gospel of Jesus Christ, to serve God, and to assist with the work of the Church. In other churches, ministers or priests are separate from the ordinary members of the congregation. Often, they study in seminaries for many years to deepen their knowledge of the scriptures and to practice the rituals they will perform for their congregations. However, when the Church was restored through Joseph Smith, the Lord instructed that this priesthood should be in every family as a means to bless the family. Through this priesthood, the father of the family, with the counsel and assistance of his wife, governs the family in accordance with the teachings of Jesus Christ, which include kindness, patience, and love. Through this priesthood, the father is entitled to receive revelation directly from the Lord for his own family. He is entitled to perform certain ordinances such as baptizing his children (with the knowledge and consent of the presiding priesthood holder of the congregation—the bishop) and to give priesthood blessings of comfort and counsel to his family. Where a single woman is the head of a family, the bishop, Elders Quorum President, and the home teachers provide support and perform those ordinances. Each week, part of the Sunday worship is devoted to priesthood meetings for the men, where they learn how to be better husbands, fathers, and individuals, and Relief Society meetings for the women, where they learn how to be better wives, mothers, and individuals.

The priesthood is divided into the Priesthood of Aaron, named after the brother of Moses, and the Priesthood of Melchizedek, the great High Priest to whom Abraham paid his tithing.[28] The Aaronic Priesthood is a "preparatory" priesthood, having the offices of Deacon, Teacher, and Priest. It is designed to school the new brother in some of the ordinances of the Church. This includes preparing and passing the sacrament each Sunday, administering or blessing the sacrament, and visiting the sick and homes of other members to befriend and help them.

The Melchizedek Priesthood includes the offices of Elder and High Priest. This higher priesthood is necessary for performing certain ordinances, such as conferring the gift of the Holy Ghost upon a newly-baptized member, giving blessings of healing, or entering the temple for the endowment ordinance. The Melchizedek Priesthood is conferred upon a new brother in the Church following a period of activity in the Church when the ward and stake Church leaders are satisfied that the brother is sufficiently spiritually mature and stable to accept the additional responsibilities of this higher priesthood. The Lord has said

28. Genesis 14:18-20.

that a brother who accepts the Melchizedek Priesthood and magnifies his calling will be sanctified by the Spirit, become the elect of God, and all that the Father has will be shared with him in the day of his judgment.[29]

Therefore, when the Lord was instructing Brother Gilbert to take upon him the ordination of Elder, he was instructing him to continue to study the scriptures, to attend Church each week, to accept and learn the duties of the Priesthood of Aaron and to prepare for and receive the office of Elder in the Melchizedek Priesthood. Through such growth and development, Brother Gilbert would be putting down his roots into the gospel soil to strengthen himself and build the Church. Brother Gilbert followed the Lord's instructions and was ordained an Elder in 1831, and later, was ordained as one of the presiding High Priests of the Church in Missouri.

And what was Brother Gilbert to do with this knowledge and priesthood authority?—Preach the gospel of faith in the Lord Jesus

---

29. Doctrine & Covenants 84: 33-38.

Christ, repentance, baptism for remission of sins, and receiving the Holy Spirit by the laying on of hands by those holding the Melchizedek Priesthood.

As a woman or young woman baptized into the Church you have your own role. While you will not be ordained to the priesthood, you will receive authority in the callings you accept and you will teach and administer in many functions alongside the brothers of the Church and in your families. Most importantly, as a sister you should understand that the Lord's instruction to Brother Gilbert to preach the gospel and be a missionary applies equally to you. This means you need to continue to study the scriptures so you can better teach the gospel to your family and friends. You have the same gift of the Holy Ghost to receive inspiration for your life and to enable you to testify in great power and authority to the truthfulness of the gospel.

As a new member of the Church, it is not necessary for you to quit your job or school and become a full-time missionary, although some single members of the Church choose to do that and some married couples serve missions after their retirement. You can serve as an effective missionary just by talking about the Church to your family and friends or going out on "team-ups" or "splits" with the full-time missionaries in your ward as they visit people they are teaching about the Church.

While it is important to study and gain knowledge so that you do not teach false doctrine, it is important to recognize that the Lord expects you to begin testifying of what you have learned from the very beginning of your membership in the Church. Sometimes, new members of the Church feel they must be in the Church for many years, or become bishops or Relief Society Presidents before they have sufficient knowledge to share the gospel with family or friends. This is not true. Learning the gospel is a life-long process and if we all waited until we were perfect in our knowledge or practice of the gospel, no one would ever share the gospel. It is also important to recognize that it is the Holy Ghost that confirms to a person that the things they are hearing are true. It is not our great learning or our eloquence that convinces or persuades others to join the Church; in fact, if they join the Church for these reasons they will soon fall away. So, even as new members of the Church, we need to begin sharing the gospel.

The Apostle Paul says we should not be ashamed of the gospel of Jesus Christ because it is the power of God unto salvation.[30] If we have love for our family and friends, we will want them to have the blessings that are promised only through obedience to the gospel. One of the things you will experience when you testify to others of the things you have learned is that the Holy Ghost will come over you as you share your testimony. This will be another spiritual experience confirming to you the correctness of your decision to join the Church and the Lord's desire that you assist in the growth of the Church by sharing the gospel.

---

30. Romans 1:16.

4 Accept a Calling
D&C 53:4

4.And also to be an agent unto this church in the place which shall be appointed by the bishop, according to commandments which shall be given hereafter.

Brother Gilbert is being instructed to be an agent unto the Church. What is an agent? In law, an agent is one who is acting on behalf of another to carry out some assignment. In the Church we call these assignments "callings." They are called "callings" because they come from the Lord through our Church leaders. The Lord has said, "This is my work and my glory— to bring to pass the immortality and eternal life of man."[31] All of our callings in the Church are to assist the Lord in that work. In a subsequent revelation, Brother Gilbert was called to administer the "Lord's storehouse," which is the collection of food and clothing from the members

---

31. Moses 1:39, The Pearl of Great Price.

of the Church to be distributed by the bishop to the poor and needy members of the Church.

The Lord says his house is a house of order and not a house of confusion.[32] This means that those who have responsibilities for leadership in the Church need the ability to coordinate all the Lord's work on earth. Within the Church there are many things the Lord has commanded us to do. In other churches, this responsibility often falls mostly or entirely on the priest, minister, or pastor of the congregation. In our Church, except for modest salaries paid to the General Authorities who devote their full-time efforts to the work of the Church, most of the work is done by the stake and ward officers. These people serve in the Church part-time without pay, while working in their secular occupations. As a result, all the work of the Church that needs to be done cannot be done by the bishop or the stake president alone. The Lord has instructed that members of the Church, including new members, should accept callings to help with the work of the Church.

---

32. Doctrine & Covenants 132:8.

Like all of the commandments of the Lord, accepting a calling brings with it blessings. Those who accept these callings to assist with the work of the Church are blessed in their personal lives; they grow strong in the gospel as they serve others. The importance of service to others cannot be over-emphasized in progressing in the gospel of Jesus Christ. Much of the sin of the world comes from selfishness. As you give time to serving others, sharing your talents, and lifting others' burdens through fulfilling your calling, the blessings of love, unity, and fellowship will be given you. Some of these callings include home teaching for men and visiting teaching for women; teaching primary children, young men, or young women; acting as greeters for meetings; preparing the Church bulletin; serving as secretaries and clerks; and the many other callings in a typical ward congregation. The Lord said, "Be one; and if ye are not one ye are not mine."[33] This unity comes to a congregation through selfless service. Those who serve in

---

33. Doctrine & Covenants 38:27.

this way find that their own burdens are lightened. Often those they serve give back in sharing information, testimony, strength, knowledge, and wisdom, and their personal confidence and skills grow.

It is very common for new members of the Church to feel reluctant to accept callings because they lack knowledge and experience in the Church. The Church is absolutely the best place for those who lack confidence to learn to serve. It is composed of the kindest, most forgiving people on the earth, all of whom have passed through the same experience as a new member of the Church, learning to serve in callings in which they had no previous experience. Just as the Lord instructed Brother Gilbert, as a new member, the place where you will be appointed to serve will be determined by the bishop of the ward. The bishop will ask you to accept a calling and will provide training, assistance, and support, directly or through his counselors or other ward leaders, to help you succeed. The calling from the bishop comes to you after an interview where the bishop assesses your skills, experience, knowledge, education, strength of testimony, availability, and other factors.

But notice the Lord says to Brother Gilbert that his calling will come "according to commandments which shall be given hereafter." The Lord is telling Brother Gilbert that his calling will be in accordance with what the Lord commands His Church leaders. In Brother Gilbert's case we know that this was fulfilled because Joseph Smith recorded a revelation instructing Brother Gilbert to establish a store and to use the profits to buy land for the needy Church members. In other words, after the bishop interviews you, he will discuss the needs of the ward with his counselors and the Lord will reveal to the bishop where the Lord wants you to serve. One of the most strengthening experiences in the gospel is to receive callings which you later realize only the Lord could have known were right for you, beyond the mere mortal wisdom of the bishop or his counselors.

Sometimes, you may be asked to serve in a calling where you have no prior experience and you feel you have no ability. It is important that you do the best you can in what you are called to do. As you work at it, studying the scriptures, seeking assistance from others, and praying to the Lord for guidance, your ability to fulfill the calling will improve. Through this, the personal growth the Lord wants you to have will occur, and the Church and the other members will be blessed. Nevertheless, you should keep the bishop informed of any change in your circumstances, such as your time availability, health, new family or work responsibilities, or other changes which may affect your ability to fulfill your calling. In some cases, the bishop may feel it is appropriate to change your calling to something more consistent with your new circumstances. Nevertheless, as Church members we should always have some calling by which we are contributing to the work of the Lord.

Lastly, continue to remember that your service in your calling is appreciated by the bishop, the other members of the Church, and, most importantly, the Lord. One of the eternal truths is that we always have our free agency to do the Lord's work or not to do it. Those who are baptized and accept callings are called "servants" and "friends" by the Lord and are promised His blessings. There will be times when fulfilling your calling is inconvenient, maybe even very difficult. This was as the Lord intended it. As we make sacrifices of our personal interests, including our time, hobbies, and friends, we are "forsaking the world" and building His Church. As all of those who have been in the Church for a long time can testify, the Lord never forgets our efforts to do His work, and sooner or later, we receive blessings beyond our expectations.

5 Follow the Church Leaders
D&C 53:5

5. And again, verily I say unto you, you shall take your journey with my servants Joseph Smith, Jun., and Sidney Rigdon.

The Lord instructs Brother Gilbert to take his journey with his servants Joseph Smith and Sidney Rigdon. This is an endorsement by the Lord that Joseph Smith and Sidney Rigdon are his authorized servants and are worthy of Brother Gilbert's allegiance. Who were Joseph Smith and Sidney Rigdon? Joseph Smith was the President of the Church and Sidney Rigdon was called by the Lord to assist Joseph. As such they were the leaders of the Church. The Lord was telling Brother Gilbert that he needed to look to them and be with them. Not all of Brother Gilbert's direction would come directly from the Lord, he needed to accept guidance from the Church leaders and support and sustain them in the Lord's work.

In Brother Gilbert's day, the body of the Church moved physically from time to time. It was originally organized and established in upstate New York. The Lord then commanded Joseph and the Church members to re-locate to the State of Ohio because there were people there that the Lord knew would accept the gospel when it was preached to them. At a later time, the Lord commanded the Church members to move to Missouri, then to Illinois, and finally, to Utah. In the early days of the Church when the number of members of the Church was small, it was very important that they be in close physical proximity to each other. Joseph was continuing to receive revelations from the Lord, which took time to implement, and he needed to be able to communicate the things he was learning to the members of the Church in instructional meetings. The modern communication methods of radio, television, e-mail, and even the telegraph, were not available to him. In addition, the members of the Church needed each other, to strengthen each other's faith by sharing their spiritual experiences, by sharing their financial means with the needy, by sharing their talents and abilities in callings, and to be a family to one another for those whose families had disowned them when they joined the Church. This work was known as the "gathering" and was prophesied from Old Testament times.[34] When Brother Gilbert received this instruction, he was living in Ohio and his challenge was to obey by physically relocating to Missouri, which he did shortly after the Prophet Joseph Smith went there.

Today, the Church is much larger and it is not necessary for each new member to relocate to Salt Lake City, Utah, the Church's headquarters. The Lord instructed Joseph Smith to establish "stakes" where the program of the Church is replicated around the world. The reasons for the gathering recited above continue, however, and Church members need to participate in wards and stakes where these goals can be achieved and blessings realized. It is extremely important for Church members to

---

34. Isaiah 11:10-16, Jeremiah 3:18, 16:14-21, I Nephi 22:4-12, 2 Nephi 10:21-22, 3 Nephi 15:13-15, 16:1-5, Doctrine & Covenants 133:26-35.

spiritually take their journey with the Church leaders, especially the Prophet and Apostles of the Church, but also the stake and ward leaders, throughout their lives. The Lord has told us He will not allow our leaders to lead us astray—He will remove them out of their positions or He will forgive us for the mistakes we make relying on their guidance. However, especially as a new member of the Church, you need to be humble and realize that you are still a child in spiritual things, no matter what the extent of your worldly education and attainments. Our Church leaders often have long years of experience in the gospel, knowledge of the scriptures and the teachings of the prophets, and wise discernment by the gift of the Holy Ghost. We need to respect their positions and accept their counsel—in this way we take our life's journey with them and the Lord can lead us and bless us.

One of the ways we can receive their counsel and follow their spiritual teachings is to attend the special meetings that occur. Periodically, you will hear of, and should attend, stake meetings where several ward congregations gather together and the stake president, the members of the High Council, and other church leaders will give counsel—not just to new members—but to all the members of the Church within the stake. Also, you will have the opportunity to listen to General Conference twice a year—in April and October—broadcast by radio, television, satellite television and Internet, where the President and Prophet of the Church, members of the Quorum of the Twelve Apostles, members of the Quorum of the Seventy, and the Relief Society, Young Men, Young Women and Primary organization leaders will speak and offer counsel.

Another thing we can learn from this instruction to Brother Gilbert relates to how he handled chastisement from the Lord through the Prophet. In one of the later revelations to Joseph Smith in the year 1833, the Lord says, "I am not well pleased with many things; and I am not well pleased with my servant William E. McLellin, neither with my servant Sidney

Gilbert...." It certainly must have been shocking to hear this rebuke from the Lord delivered by the Prophet Joseph Smith in a written revelation that all the Church members could read. Brother Gilbert could have easily felt that he had made many sacrifices for the Lord and His Church and that he did not deserve this chastisement. In subsequent revelations the Lord told the Prophet Joseph Smith:

Verily, thus saith the Lord unto you whom I love, and whom I also chasten that their sins may be forgiven, for with the chastisement I prepare a way for their deliverance in all things out of temptation, and I have loved you, Wherefore ye must needs be chastened and stand rebuked before my face.[35]

For all those who will not endure chastening, but deny me, cannot be sanctified.[36]

[H]e that will not bear chastisement is not worthy of my kingdom.[37]

---

35. Doctrine & Covenants 95:1-2.
36. Doctrine & Covenants 101:5.
37. Doctrine & Covenants 136:31.

To Brother Gilbert's credit, he did not quit the Church. He bore his public chastisement from the Lord patiently and continued to follow the Church leaders and do better in his obedience to the gospel.

Like Brother Gilbert, and all other members of the Church, as a new member there will certainly come times when you feel like you are being criticized, perhaps, in the way you fulfilled your calling or kept one of the commandments. You may feel you do not deserve the criticism or chastisement. It is extremely important that you keep the foregoing revelations in mind. If the chastisement comes from another member of the Church, you can consider it for whatever value or truth it may contain, but you need not regard it as coming from the Lord. Unfortunately, many new members of the Church stop participating in the Church because of some intentional or unintentional comment or criticism from another member of the Church. If the chastisement comes from your bishop or the leader of the organization in which you have a calling, you should take it more seriously and seek to understand their dissatisfaction and how you can improve. This is the process of sanctification and perfection. The Lord said, "Be ye therefore perfect." This can only happen as you accept correction from the Lord's appointed servants. Their correction will be in the spirit of love and forgiveness. They do not desire to offend you, but you must have the courage and fortitude to press forward and overcome any resentment that may arise within you when such correction is given.

6 Receive the Higher Ordinances of the Gospel
D&C 53:6

6. Behold, these are the first ordinances which you shall receive; and the residue shall be made known in a time to come, according to your labor in the vineyard.

As a new member of the Church, Brother Gilbert had received certain ordinances. These included baptism, confirmation for the gift of the Holy Ghost, and membership in the Church. The Lord had also instructed him to prepare to receive the ordinance of ordination to the Melchizedek Priesthood.

But the Lord indicates that there are other ordinances that will be made known to him in a time to come. These ordinances include receiving a patriarchal blessing and receiving endowments and sealings in the temple. In 1834, three years after this revelation, Brother Gilbert was among several men who were specifically "called, chosen and appointed" by the Lord in a revelation to receive their endowment in the temple.

A patriarchal blessing is a blessing given by a person within each stake of the Church called a patriarch. The Lord instructed Joseph Smith to ordain patriarchs with priesthood authority for the blessing of the members of the Church. Each new member should make an appointment with the patriarch and, after proper fasting and prayer, meet with him to receive this priesthood blessing. It will be administered by the patriarch placing his hands on your head (the laying on of hands), and will be recorded and a copy provided to you in writing for your continuing review and study. The patriarchal blessing is a revelation from the Lord to you, just as Section 53 was a revelation to Brother Gilbert from the Lord. In your blessing, the Lord will reveal those things that He wants you to know. Sometimes, this will include your potential as the Lord knows you from long association in the spirit world prior to your birth in mortality, your spiritual lineage, and, if you continue faithful in the gospel, promises of blessings to be fulfilled in this life or after your resurrection.

There are other ordinances that you should prepare to receive in the temples of the Lord. These include the endowment and sealings. An endowment is a gift and blessing from the Lord. It consists of additional knowledge regarding the purpose of life and promises from the Lord to you through the priesthood officiators in the temple pertaining to this life and your life after the resurrection. The endowment is necessary for the higher degree of salvation called exaltation. It carries with it additional blessings the Lord has promised to those who fully dedicate themselves to the work of the Lord. Sealings are ordinances by which men and women marry for "time and all eternity," so their marriage relationship lasts beyond the resurrection, instead of "until death do you part" as in civil marriages. Parents may also be sealed to children. It is important to understand that sealings are always subject to the worthiness and free agency of the parties. No couple or children will be entitled to the blessings of these family relationships after the resurrection unless they have been obedient to the teachings of Jesus Christ throughout their lives and, after the resurrection, continue to choose to be together.

Why did the Lord tell Brother Gilbert that these things would be made known to him "according to his labor in my vineyard"? The Lord told Brother Gilbert this because the temple endowment ordinance commits those who accept it to full dedication to the work of the Church throughout their lives. This is a decision that should not be taken lightly. Consequently, no matter how enthusiastic or knowledgeable you may be when you first join the Church, you are required to wait at least a year before you can go to the temple to receive your endowment. This gives you a chance to more fully experience the Church—the blessings, as well as the adversities and obstacles Satan will put into your life. Then, when you are capable of making an informed judgment of whether you want to continue in this

Church through all of your life, you will be sufficiently spiritually mature to enter the temple. You should also understand that you will need to comply with the commandments of the gospel in order to be worthy to enter the temple. If there have been lapses in your obedience to those commandments, it will usually require additional time before you have "forsaken the world," overcome your addictions, and strengthened your knowledge and faith through scripture reading and fulfilling your callings. Entering into the temple for your endowment is a mutual decision between the bishop and you as to when you are ready. You should also be aware that you can attend the temple to participate in baptisms for your ancestors as a way to become familiar with the temple. This can occur even as a new member of the Church without waiting one year, provided you are obeying the teachings of the gospel.

7 Endure to the End
D&C 53:7

7. And again, I would that ye should learn that he only is saved who endureth unto the end. Even so. Amen.

In the final verse of the revelation, the Lord tells Brother Gilbert that he must continue in obedience to the requirements of the gospel until the end of his life in order to obtain salvation, that is, to return and live in the presence of God in the celestial kingdom. In following and sustaining the Church leaders, the time came in Jackson County, Missouri where the leaders of the Church were enduring much persecution. Brother Gilbert was one of six men who offered to be scourged or even give his life if the mob would cease its persecution, but the mob refused. On another occasion, the mobbers put several guns to Brother Gilbert's chest and two were fired, but through the blessing of God, they both misfired and he received no injury. After thus proving he was willing to die for the gospel, it was not long before the Lord took Brother Gilbert to Himself. In 1834, a group of Church members came to Missouri. Many of them were sick with cholera. In Christian compassion Brother Gilbert took them into his home. Fourteen died from the disease, including Brother Gilbert.

Often, in our own undertakings in life, we are enthusiastic and diligent in the beginning, but our efforts fade as time goes on. Although the Lord appreciates all the good things we do during our lives, and will reward us accordingly, the fullest blessings are reserved for those who, in patient obedience, continue in the gospel and Church activity throughout their lives. The Lord tells us that those who make covenants with Him in baptism and in the temple and then fail to fulfill them have no promise of eternal life.[38] He tells us those who are not "valiant" in their testimony of Jesus

---

38. Doctrine & Covenants 82:10.

Christ receive only the second or terrestrial degree of glory in the judgment day, rather than living in the presence of God the Father in the celestial glory.[39] Just as importantly, he warns that those who "altogether turn away" from the covenants and promises they have made in receiving the Melchizedek Priesthood will not have forgiveness in this world nor the world to come.[40]

Continuation in gospel activity, however, is not a burden to be endured. It is a blessing that the Lord promises will bring us peace in this life and eternal life in the world to come.[41] It is a lifestyle that brings greater happiness in this life and after our resurrection than any other lifestyle can bring. Consequently, those who obey the teachings of the gospel find that any other lifestyle becomes repugnant and disappointing. Although, there are times when we lack faith in our ability to live certain requirements of the gospel and we suffer setbacks, the Lord is merciful and quick to forgive. As long as

39. Doctrine & Covenants 76:79.
40. Doctrine & Covenants 84:41.
41. Doctrine & Covenants 59:23.

we are trying our best, the Lord gives us enlightenment, faith, wisdom, and success in living the gospel.

None of us know whether our time on this earth will be long or short. Whatever time we are allotted, this is the time for us to prove our faithfulness to the gospel and the Lord has instructed us to endure to the end. The prophets have told us that He does not give us commandments we cannot keep,[42] and that God will not permit Satan to tempt us beyond that which we are able to bear.[43]

---

42. I Nephi 3:7, The Book of Mormon;
43. I Corinthians 10:13, Alma 13:28, The Book of Mormon.

CONCLUSION

The Prophet Malachi has said:

[A] book of remembrance was written before Him for them that feared the Lord, and that thought upon His name. And they shall be mine saith the Lord of hosts, in that day when I make up my jewels.[44]

The Lord refers to you as His jewel to communicate how precious you are to Him. The day that the Lord takes up his jewels will be the day of His Second Coming, or our resurrection. He has said that in the day of judgment He will say to those who have served Him:

Well done thou good and faithful servant . . . Enter thou into the joy of the Lord.[45]

---

44. Malachi 3:16-17; see also 3 Nephi 24:16-17, The Book of Mormon; Doctrine & Covenants 60:4, 101:3.
45. Matthew 25:21, 23.

He has further said:

Eye hath not seen, nor ear heard, neither have entered into the heart of man, the things which God hath prepared for them that love Him.[46]

In other words, you cannot even imagine the blessings you will receive if you faithfully keep His commandments.

Finally, He has said:

Verily, verily I say unto you, ye are little children, and ye have not as yet understood how great blessings the Father hath in His own hands and prepared for you; And ye cannot bear all things now; nevertheless, be of good cheer, for I will lead you along. The kingdom is yours and the blessings thereof are yours, and the riches of eternity are yours.[47]

---

46. I Corinthians 2:9; see also Isaiah 64:9, Doctrine & Covenants 76:10.
47. Doctrine & Covenants 78:17-18.

With such promises from the Lord to encourage you, you can understand the feelings of Joseph Smith:

"[S]hall we not go on in so great a cause? Go forward and not backward. Courage . . . and on, on to the victory! Let your hearts rejoice and be exceedingly glad.[48]

At the end of our days let us be able to say, like the Apostle Paul:

I have fought a good fight, I have finished my course, I have kept the faith: Henceforth there is laid up for me a crown of righteousness, which the Lord the righteous judge, shall give me at that day; and not to me only, but unto all them that love His appearing.[49]

May it be so, I pray in the name of Jesus Christ, Amen.

Thomas E. Johnson

---

48. Doctrine & Covenants 128:22.
49. 2 Timothy 4:7-8.

About the Author

Thomas E. Johnson is an attorney, originally from Nephi, Utah, who has been living in Chicago for the past 30 years. He attended Snow College, the University of Utah and Northwestern University. He served a mission for The Church of Jesus Christ of Latter-day Saints in Japan. He is a former bishop and stake president in The Church of Jesus Christ of Latter-day Saints. He is married to Norma Lee Christensen and they have five children—Mary Melinda, Elisabeth, Eve, Susanna and Heidi.